DATE DUE

Demco No. 62-0549

Genetic **Engineering**

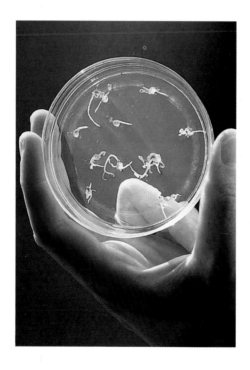

Jenny Bryan

Thomson Learning • New York

Global Issues
Genetic Engineering
Terrorism
UN—Peacekeeper?

Cover picture: A scientist removes a sample of human DNA from a plastic tube containing white blood cells.
Title page picture: Close-up of a petri dish containing genetically engineered seedlings.

Consultants:
Dr. Eric Juengst, Center for Biomedical Ethics, Case Western Reserve University, Cleveland, Ohio
Dr. Robert Whittle, Senior Lecturer in Genetics at the University of Sussex, England

First published in the United States in 1995 by
Thomson Learning, 115 Fifth Avenue,
New York, NY 10003

Published simultaneously in Great Britain by Wayland (Publishers) Ltd.

Library of Congress Cataloging-in-Publication Data
Bryan, Jenny.
Genetic engineering / Jenny Bryan.
   p.   cm.—(Global issues series)
   Includes bibliographical references and index.
   ISBN 1-56847-268-4
   1. Genetic engineering—Juvenile literature.
   [1. Genetic engineering. 2. Genetics.] I. Title. II. Series.
   QH437.5.B78   1995
   575.1'0724—dc20   94-23960

Printed in Italy

Picture Acknowledgments
Camera Press 29; Howard J. Davies 52; Mary Evans 7, 42, 58; Photri 10, 28, 40 (J. Kirby), 57, 59 (© 1990 L. Riess); Ronald Grant Archives 55 (© 1993 Universal & Amblin); Science Photo Library *cover* (P. Plailly), *title page.*(Weiss/Jerrican), *contents page* (P. Menzel), 4 (P. Plailly/Eurelios), 8 (L. Georgia), 11 (A. Barrington), 12 (P. Plailly), 13 (Dr. G. Murti), 14 (Biophoto Associates), 15 (H. Morgan), 16 (CNRI), 18 (M. Clarke), 21 (D. Parker), 22 (C. Goldin), 24 (P. Menzel), 25 (Secchi-Lecaque-Roussel-UCLAF), (J. C. Revy) 30 (below), 31 (P. Menzel) & 32, 33 (Dr. R. Stepney), 37 (H. Young), 39 (C. Pouedras), 43 (Dr. L. D. Simon), 45 (P. Plailly), 50 (Dept. of Clinical Cytogenetics, Addenbrookes Hospital, Cambridge, UK), 53 (B. Krassovsky), 54 (L. Williams), 56 (A. Pasteka), 60 (J. C. Revy); Skjold 4; Tony Stone Worldwide 27 (D. Austen), 34 (B. Ayers), 44 (P. Matson); Topham 19, 23, 46 (M. Elias/POOL), 47; Wayland 5, 6 (both), 17, 48, 49 (J. Davey), 51 (APM); Wellcome National Medical Slide Bank 30 (above), 35; Zefa 36.

CONTENTS

These lambs have inherited a human gene that was put into the DNA (deoxyribonucleic acid) of their mothers. It will make the lambs produce a protein in their milk that humans need to make their lungs work properly. People who do not make the protein get a lung disease called emphysema, which can be fatal. Thanks to sheep like these, they can now have injections of the protein.

A GENETIC REVOLUTION

On farms all over the world, thousands of animals and plants are being raised with genes that their ancestors never had. There are Australian sheep with genes to make them more wooly, Scottish ewes that produce a chemical in their milk that makes human blood clot, and Dutch cattle with extra proteins to help fight infection. Before long, we'll have sweeter tasting lettuce and tomatoes—all thanks to genetic engineering.

Sheep, cattle, chickens, pigs, fish, many other animals, and some plants have all been the subjects of genetic engineering over the last 20 years. This is just the beginning. Hardly a week goes by without an important new discovery. Within the next 20 years, scientists may well have a complete map of all the genes on the 23 pairs of chromosomes in human cells. Already, they have taken the first hesitant steps toward human gene therapy—attempting to correct abnormal genes in people with life-threatening genetic illnesses.

How far can scientists go? How far *should* they go? Which diseases should they treat? If they can cure cancer or heart disease, will it also be possible to adjust types of human behavior that some parts of society find difficult to deal with? If genetic altering of humans is found to be possible, should we allow it?

Life as we know it

All forms of life on Earth owe their physical appearance and basic instincts to the genes they inherit from their parents. From the simplest, single-celled bacteria to the most complex animals, our genes are what make us tick. Every movement human beings make, every word we say, every thought that comes into our heads is possible only because the genes in our cells are hard at work telling our bodies what to do.

Merino sheep have very thick coats. Genetic engineering allows other breeds to produce large amounts of wool, too.

The idea of changing genes to get a better yield from crops and domesticated animals is not new. For at least six thousand years, humans have been aware that certain physical characteristics are passed from one generation to the next. The first herdsmen tried to weed out the weakest animals by breeding only from their strongest, biggest, or bravest beasts. Farmers tried to improve the quality of crops by sowing seeds from only the healthiest plants.

They were, in a sense, trying to help nature along. For millions of years, those members of a species that are the best adapted to their environment are the ones that have survived. Other less well-adapted members of the same species are less able to compete for such essentials as food and territory and so die out.

Similarly, species that have been unable to adapt to changing environmental conditions have died out. Better-adapted or more adaptable species have taken their place. The naturalist Charles Darwin (1809–82), whose ideas form the basis of our current understanding of evolution, called this process natural selection.

When Charles Darwin was asked to account for his scientific success he drew attention to his "love of science, unbounded patience in long reflecting over any subject, industry in observing and collecting facts, and a fair share of invention as well as of common sense."

Our attempts to enhance natural selection have gradually become more sophisticated since Austrian monk Gregor Johann Mendel (1822–84) published his theories on genetic inheritance in 1866. He proposed that each physical characteristic is controlled by a pair of genes, one from each parent. One gene may be dominant over the other, or they may carry equal force in deciding what happens.

It may take only one gene to control the structure of a simple protein for, say, muscle fibers. Most characteristics, however, result from complicated interactions between many different genes. For example, there are many different genes involved in determining whether we are short or tall. Even then, genetics merely establishes a range of possibilities; other factors, such as diet, are also important.

Gregor Mendel is said to have cultivated and tested some 28,000 plants in order to develop his theories. In recent years, some doubt has been cast over how much research he did, but his theories still form the basis of modern genetics.

A cartoon from 1861 giving an inaccurate view of Darwin's theory. Darwin said that humans evolved from apes. The cartoonist is saying that this means that one day apes will become like humans.

These Douglas fir seedlings were grown from single cells in the laboratory. They are being nurtured under carefully controlled light and temperature conditions until they are ready to be planted in the forest. These and thousands of similar trees would not exist without the remarkable new techniques of biotechnology.

Twentieth-century scientists have gone far beyond what even the most skilled farmers have managed to do with plants and animals. They have learned how to change the ingredients that go into our genetic makeup. It isn't easy. So far, nearly all the experiments have been on microorganisms, plants, and animals; very few have involved humans.

In most cases, only one of the thousands of genes in an animal's cells has been changed. For example, to try to make Australian sheep produce more wool, scientists changed only the gene that affects the structure of the protein keratin, which humans have in their hair and nails and sheep have in their wool.

In 1974, a group of leading geneticists imposed a temporary ban on genetic engineering experiments. The science was in its early years and there were concerns about the possible dangers, such as creating public health hazards with genetically altered viruses and bacteria, or causing an ecological catastrophe by releasing altered organisms into the environment. Since then, the restrictions on genetic engineering have become more relaxed as knowledge of the science has increased and the true risks are better understood.

66 99

• • •

Early fears
In 1974, geneticists called for caution within their own field: "…our concern is based on judgements of potential rather than demonstrated risk since there are few available experimental data on the hazards of such DNA molecules and adherence to our major recommendations will entail postponement or possibly abandonment of certain types of scientifically worthwhile experiments… Nonetheless, our concern for the possible unfortunate consequences of indiscriminate application of these techniques motivates us to urge all scientists working in this area to join us in agreeing not to initiate experiments…" [1]

All genetic engineering experiments still have to be approved by government committees before they can be carried out. Inspectors check laboratories to see that geneticists are following government rules.

Who is to say how far genetic engineers should be allowed to go in the future? Most scientists are as concerned as the public that their experiments are acceptable to society. They have been brought up with the same social and moral influences as the rest of us. They want society to set the rules by which they operate. Nevertheless, few of us fully understand what is involved in their experiments. So how can we give an informed opinion?

We can only affect the way in which genetic engineering is carried out in the twenty-first century by understanding what is already done and where this could lead. If we take no interest now, we cannot complain if experiments or practices we do not like are carried out in the future. We need to be able to give informed opinions to shape the future of genetic engineering.

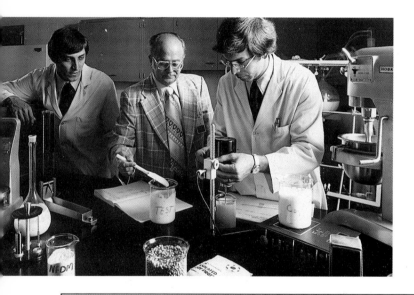

Scientists are using genetic engineering to improve the yield of many plant sources of protein, such as soy beans.

Media Watch

Freak animals

The dangers that the early critics of genetic engineering warned about have simply not happened. Crazed monsters, half human, half animal, have not broken out of the laboratories. However, in an August 1992 letter to the U.S. Food and Drug Administration, the Council for Responsible Genetics listed several cases of biotechnical experiments that did not go exactly as planned.

"When growth hormone genes were inserted into pigs, faster growth did not result (unless the animals are fed a special diet) and—irrespective of feed—creates genetically-based abnormalities such as muscle weakness, lameness, infertility, ulcers, and lethargy." [2]

"Those in the scientific community...would do well to remember that, though Frankenstein was, in fact, the scientist, virtually everyone thinks it is the name of the monster." [3]

HOW DID WE GET HERE ?

American biochemist James D. Watson (left) and British molecular biologist Francis H. C. Crick in 1953, with their model of part of a DNA molecule. They shared the 1962 Nobel Prize for Physiology or Medicine with British biophysicist Maurice H. F. Wilkins who, with the late Rosalind Franklin at King's College, London, provided much of the technical support that made the discovery possible.

The discovery that made modern genetic engineering possible came in 1953. Working together in Cambridge, England, two scientists, James D. Watson and Francis H. C. Crick, proposed the structure of DNA, an acid that carries the genetic code.

People already knew that we inherit the basic blueprint for our physical and mental makeup in the form of genes from our parents. They also knew that there are thousands of genes sitting on the 23 pairs of chromosomes in the nucleus of each of our cells. What they did not know is how this information is stored or how the body uses it. For example, how does the body know when to replace worn-out skin cells? Where does it get the materials? How does each skin cell know where to grow and what to do?

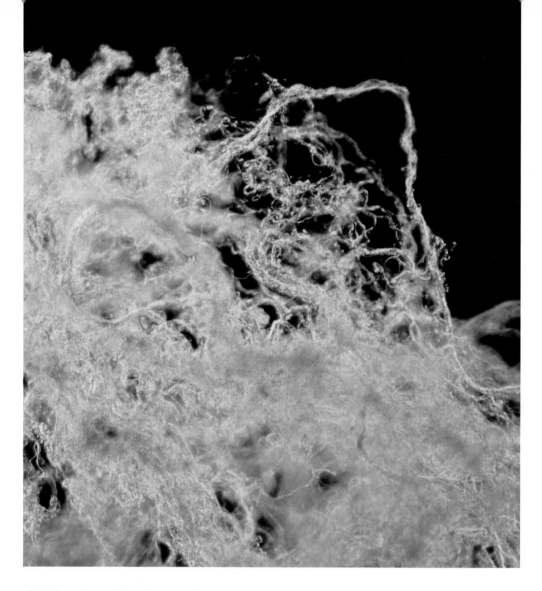

DNA from human blood cells. DNA is found in nearly all living cells and holds the genetic code to life.

The answer lies in a complicated system of protein chemical messengers that rush around the body telling it what to do. There are chief messengers, which tell whole organs, such as the heart, what to do. There are senior messengers, which tell cells what to do, and there are junior messengers, which work inside cells and control day-to-day tasks, such as making energy from nutrients.

Where do these messengers come from? The body has to make them. They are small pieces of protein called peptides. The building blocks of the peptides are called amino acids, and there are 20 different types. So, where do the amino acids come from? In 1953, Watson and Crick showed that something called deoxyribonucleic acid (DNA), which makes up the chromosomes in every plant and animal cell, holds the answers.

DNA molecules are made up of hundreds, thousands, and sometimes even millions of smaller units joined together. Think of a strand of DNA as a necklace of multicolored beads. Each sequence of three "beads" holds the code for an amino acid. When the sequence is switched on, an amino acid is made. At any one time, thousands of "beads" will be switched on, busily ordering amino acids to be made and linked together to form peptides.

Genes aren't being decoded to make amino acids all the time, so there have to be control mechanisms. On each side of a gene are other "beads" that switch it on and off.

Plasmids of DNA from the bacterium *Escherichia coli* (color has been added to make them more visible). This plasmid, called PBR 322, is the one most commonly used in genetic engineering. (Magnified more than 40,000 times.)

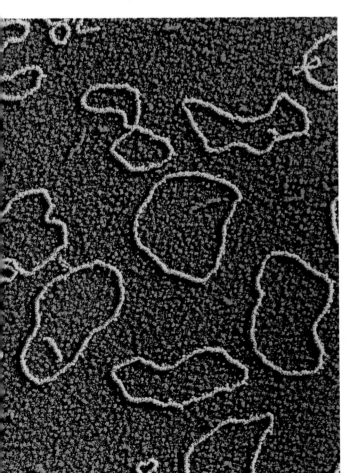

Even DNA that does not code for specific proteins may prove very useful to scientists by acting as signposts on the chromosomes to show where specific genes are found.

As soon as scientists understood the structure of genes and how to decode them, they started thinking about changing them. Before they could do that, they needed to put together "maps" of genes in the DNA of different animals.

They started with the simplest microbes. Their favorite was a bacterium called *Escherichia coli*, shortened to *E. coli*. It has only a fraction of the amount of DNA found in human cells but, like other bacteria, its DNA is spread out through the cell. (DNA is only held in the nuclei of animal cells.) *E. coli* has rings, or loops, of DNA called plasmids. They have turned out to be ideal tools for genetic engineering.

Cloning genes

In 1973, two U.S. scientists, Dr. Stanley Cohen and Dr. Herbert Boyer, announced that they had managed to put together a working piece of DNA made from genes from two different *E. coli* microbes.

Threadlike human chromosomes carry all the genes needed to make human proteins. Chromosomes are found in the nucleus at the center of a cell. Each chromosome is made up of two strands (chromatids) joined in a region known as the centromere.

They cut open a plasmid from one *E. coli* and inserted some DNA from another *E. coli*. They then put the mixed plasmid back into the *E. coli* cells. The cells worked normally, reproducing and also decoding to make amino acids. The scientists had successfully cloned genes: they had produced *E. coli* with exactly the same mixed plasmid as the original parent cell. The era of genetic engineering had begun.

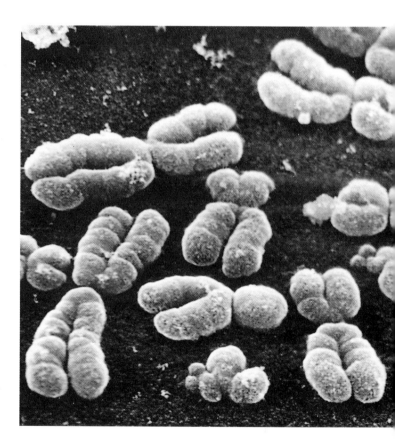

Things happened very fast after that. Other scientists copied Cohen and Boyer's crucial experiments. Before long, they were putting DNA from different microbes into *E. coli*. Soon, they put animal DNA into bacterial cells. Then they tried to put DNA from one animal into cells of a different animal. This was unsuccessful, because animal cells do not have plasmids of DNA like bacteria. Scientists had to think of something else.

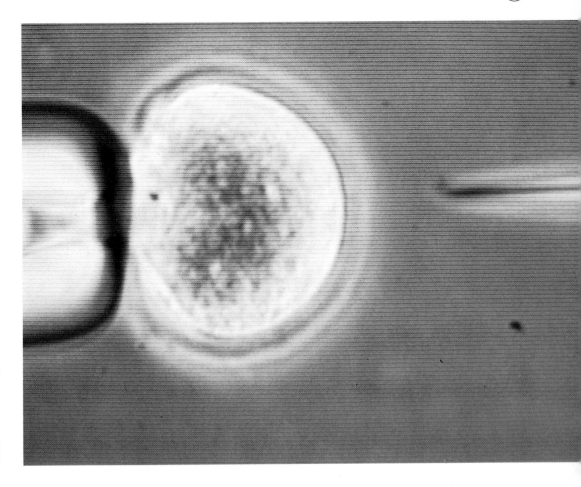

"Mighty Mouse"

In 1982, Drs. Richard Palmiter and Ralph Brinster, and their teams from the Universities of Washington and Pennsylvania, announced that they had successfully transferred the gene for rat growth hormone into the DNA of a mouse. The foreign gene worked in the mouse, and "Mighty Mouse"—as it was nicknamed—grew to twice the size of an ordinary mouse.

Getting the gene into the mouse cells was no mean feat. Scientists used a needle with a tip just 1/1,000 of a millimeter across to inject the rat genes directly into fertilized mouse eggs. They chose their moment very carefully. The gene was put in after the egg had been fertilized by a sperm, but before the nuclei of the egg and sperm had fused. Remarkably, the foreign DNA was built into the chromosomes of the new embryo.

Foreign DNA being injected into a cell through a tiny needle in an incredibly delicate operation. The work is done under a microscope and watched on a CRT screen. The dark area in the center of the cell is the nucleus.

Since Palmiter and Brinster's crucial experiment, scientists have found other ways to create so-called "transgenic" species—animals with DNA from more than one species. Nature could never have done this on its own. Animals mate only within their own species. DNA from a human cell never gets near DNA from a cow or a pig. Even if it did, they would not normally mix. Only in carefully controlled laboratory conditions can genes from different species be persuaded not just to mix but also to switch on and work normally.

The closest nature gets to genetic engineering is during viral infection. Viruses, such as those that spread colds, flu, or hepatitis, can insert their own DNA into that of an animal cell. Days, months, or even years later, the viral DNA switches on and the viral peptides that are produced attack their host. Scientists have taken note of such a useful natural method of genetic engineering and often use viruses to transfer DNA between humans (see page 43).

The human immunodeficiency virus (HIV), shown here in color for clarity, is believed to cause AIDS. AIDS wreaks havoc in the cells of the human immune system, leaving the cells incapable of protecting the person from even the most minor infection. (Magnified more than 100,000 times.)

Viruses have also been useful in putting genes into plant cells. Not only do plant cells have no plasmid DNA, they also have tough outer walls made of cellulose, which are hard to penetrate. Plant bacteria and viruses, however, can get in. So scientists have used these to transfer genes to protect plants and trees from infection and to protect fruit and vegetables from the effects of frost and snow. In the same way, tomatoes have been altered so that they do not produce the gas ethylene, which causes them to ripen naturally. When artificially exposed to the gas—at a time that suits the wholesaler—the tomatoes ripen. Other fruits and vegetables have been engineered to stay ripe longer. Two companies, ICI and Calgene, have produced such a tomato by altering the effects of the gene for the chemical that causes rotting.

Sweeter, more flavorful vegetables will soon be on the market if genetic engineers have their way. But are we being told enough about what is done to our food?

Media Watch

Fruits and vegetables

Genetically engineered fruits and vegetables are already on sale in some countries, often without labels to say what has happened to them. Some people object. In 1992, the debate focused on tomatoes. Jeremy Rifkin of the Pure Food Campaign claimed:

"This is very, very serious. This is going to be the consumer issue of the 1990s, and the marketplace is going to reject all genetic tampering with food. The tomato is just the beginning of a global debate…Think of that tomato; it rots for a reason, as part of the natural cycle of life on this planet. These people are going to interrupt that process for commercial gain. When people realize the implications of that, they are going to say this is a border we will not cross." 4

At the same time, Calgene's Bill Hiatt said of his work:

"DNA is a universal alphabet, a four letter alphabet. A gene is a word made up of that alphabet, and a chromosome is made up of genes, like a sentence. What we have done with the tomato is remove one word from an existing sentence…I really don't believe that what I have been doing for twenty years is dangerous." 5

Microbes as factories

The first practical use for genetic engineering was to turn bacteria into factories to make proteins that were useful to humans. The first important product to come off the production line was insulin.

Insulin is a hormone that controls the amount of sugar we have in our blood. Other animals have it, too. People with diabetes do not make enough insulin and, without treatment, their sugar levels can rise too high, leading in some cases to death. Many diabetics need injections of insulin every day. They used to inject small quantities of insulin taken from pigs, sheep, or cattle. It worked well for most people, but some people reacted badly to it.

Now, people with diabetes can inject human insulin made in bacteria. The gene for human insulin is put into the DNA of *E. coli* and switched on. The bacteria produce large quantities of human insulin. This is taken out of the bacteria and carefully purified before being used to treat diabetes. Since it is human insulin, it works better than animal insulin and has fewer side effects.

Insulin was just the first life-giving substance to be made by genetic engineering. Since then, scientists have used bacteria and animal cells to make many other important proteins. They include factor VIII (a protein needed for blood to clot) and human growth hormone.

Daily insulin injections help keep the amount of sugar in this girl's blood under control. The genetically engineered insulin she is injecting works exactly the same way as naturally produced insulin.

Genetic fingerprinting was used as evidence in the case of athlete and commentator O.J. Simpson, accused of murder in 1994. U.S. states are quickly building genetic fingerprint files on convicted criminals, just as files of fingerprints were originally compiled earlier this century.

Genetic engineering has had many spin-offs. Today, it is one part of an area of science called biotechnology.

Genetic fingerprinting

The "Battersea Beast" was jailed for 20 years in 1992 for the rape and robbery of five London women. His case was widely reported. It took three and a half years to catch him. He ended up behind bars thanks to a revolutionary new technique called genetic fingerprinting.

Genetic fingerprinting was developed by British scientist Professor Alec Jeffreys during the mid-1980s at Leicester University. The technique has helped to track down hundreds of murderers, rapists, burglars, and muggers from traces of blood or other body fluids left behind at the scene of the crime. Before genetic fingerprinting was available, scientists had to rely on identifying certain proteins in blood or body fluids.

In some cases the tests were accurate enough to
put criminals behind bars or to settle paternity or
maternity cases. All too often, however, the results
were uncertain.

Through genetic fingerprinting, the "Battersea Beast"
was identified from 900 possible suspects. His unique
pattern of DNA gave him away. Just as all people have
a different pattern of lines on the skin of their
fingertips, they also have a unique pattern of DNA.

Genetic fingerprinting works like this. DNA is
extracted from the cells in a drop of blood. It is divided
into separate strands. An enzyme is then used to chop
the DNA into pieces of different lengths. Imagine,
again, the DNA as a necklace of beads: the enzyme cuts
very specifically between particular "beads." Since
everyone has a different pattern of DNA, no two people
will have exactly the same set of matching fragments of
DNA.

DNA samples from different sources can be treated in
this way. The thousands of different fragments created
by the cutting action of enzymes can be sorted by size,
transferred onto a fabric membrane, and stained so that
they can be easily read. The result looks similar to the
bar codes on store items. This is the genetic fingerprint.
No two people will have the same pattern.

If the DNA pattern of a sample of blood or body fluid
left at the scene of a crime matches that from a blood
sample taken from a suspect, it is likely that the
suspect is, in fact, guilty of the crime.

Genetic fingerprinting is now used in many countries as
a part of immigration procedures for people claiming a
right of citizenship because they are related to people
already living in the country they want to move to.
Scientists look for similarities in their genetic
fingerprints. A child inherits half of its DNA from one
parent and half from the other. So its DNA fingerprint
should resemble part of its mother's and part of its
father's genetic fingerprint. By conducting thousands of
tests, scientists have worked out statistically the

They may look like the bar
codes on a cereal box, but
these DNA pictures can
help prove whether or not
two people are related.

chances of individuals with very similar genetic
fingerprints being related. But DNA tests are costly and
can take a long time—more money and effort than most
nations are willing to spend on prospective immigrants.

In Argentina, scientists are using DNA fingerprinting to help reunite parents with their children
who were stolen during the former military regime. DNA from blood samples of likely relatives
is compared with that from a lost child. Many desperate parents who could not recognize their
children, because they had not seen them since they were babies, have been helped in this way.

These spaniels may look like pedigree animals, but the only way to be sure is to DNA fingerprint them.

Genetic fingerprinting can help to settle paternity cases. If a man denies that he is the father of a child and refuses to support it, a blood test can show whether he is telling the truth. Animal breeders even use the test to prove whether or not a potential prize-winning puppy was fathered by a pedigree dog or is the result of a mongrel mating.

Room for error?

Unfortunately, the results of genetic fingerprinting are not always as clear-cut as scientists would like. In criminal cases, scientists generally use four different DNA tests on each sample, which gives them eight different bands of genetic information to compare. Sometimes five or six of the bands match but two or three are very slightly different. Scientists then calculate statistically the chances of the two samples not coming from the same person. But there's a problem: there are several different ways of doing the calculation. One may show that the chance of the samples coming from different people are ten million to one, another that the chances are fifty million to one.

Blood is being removed from these trousers for analysis to find out if it comes from a murder victim or the person who killed him. The analysis may help detectives to track down the murderer.

Both figures sound very impressive, but what happens if the suspect insists that he or she is innocent and can show that he or she was somewhere else when the crime was committed? Would you trust science or would you trust the other evidence in front of you?

Genetic fingerprinting has been used very successfully in hundreds of legal cases since it was first introduced in the late 1980s. Nevertheless, in a handful of cases, the evidence it gave has turned out to be uncertain. Inevitably, this has raised questions about how reliable it is.

When there is a danger that a murderer may walk free or an innocent person might spend many years in prison, there has to be no shadow of a doubt. That's why some countries want to see further work on genetic fingerprinting before they will rely on it completely.

66   99

• • •

Acceptable evidence?
Genetic fingerprinting has proved a valuable aid to identification. "I defy anybody to give me two DNA samples from people other than identical twins where I cannot easily and repeatedly distinguish them," [6] claimed Professor Alec Jeffreys, who developed the technique, in 1990. However, the fact that DNA testing may not always give the correct result has raised doubts about its acceptability as court evidence. "DNA evidence is not infallible. All laboratory work is subject to error; and…a witness or prosecutor will seldom (if ever) be justified in stating that the probability that a reported DNA match involves someone other than the suspect is so low as to make the possibility entirely implausible." [7]

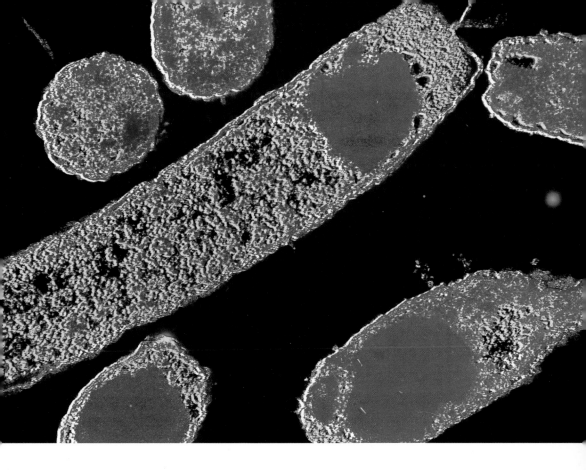

GENES FOR SALE

In December 1980, Stanford University and the University of California, both in California, were granted a broad patent to establish their ownership of the techniques of splicing (joining) and cloning genes, which are essential to all genetic engineering. Four years later, they were granted a second patent covering DNA molecules that contain the foreign genes needed to make proteins in bacteria.

This means that, until 1997, any company wanting to use genetic engineering to make drugs, chemicals, or other products must pay a fee to the two universities because their scientists, Cohen and Boyer, made these crucial discoveries. Since the early 1980s, millions of dollars have been paid. Cohen and Boyer have not become rich from their discoveries. They gave up their rights to the money to their respective California universities, where it has helped to fund many projects.

These *E. coli* bacteria (dyed for clarity) are making human interleukin-2, a naturally occurring substance that researchers sometimes use in cancer treatment. In the picture, the pink areas are the interleukin. (Magnified more than 16,000 times.)

Why shouldn't they make money? Every day, hundreds of scientists patent their discoveries in physics, chemistry, engineering, biology, and medicine. This means they register the fact that they discovered something before anyone else did.

You can't patent just any wild idea. You have to show not only that it is new, but that it has a specific use. For example, if you made a new type of metal tubing, you would have to show exactly what it could be used for.

If the patent office in a country grants you a patent, your discovery is protected within that country. If other people want to use it they must pay you. A patent does not last forever. Countries have different patent laws, but a patent does not usually last for more than 20 years. After that, anyone can freely use your discovery.

Thousands of discoveries in genetic engineering have now been patented. Some scientists feel that patenting has gone too far. They believe that DNA should not be thought of in the same way as, say, a new type of metal tubing. They argue that since it is the basis of life, no one should own it.

Patenting a discovery can also slow down the transfer of information among scientists. It can take many months for a country's patent office to decide whether to grant a patent. During this time, the scientist cannot talk about his or her discovery at a conference or publish the results, because the research might be copied before it is protected by a patent. This means that announcements about important new discoveries can be delayed. Scientists may waste time and money trying to discover things that have already been discovered elsewhere. Or they may have to stop work on something because they find that it is already protected by a patent.

In 1992 a U.S. company was granted a patent over all genetically engineered cotton. The company used a bacterium to transfer genes into the cotton plant, but the patent meant that the company also had rights over cotton produced using other genetic engineering techniques. In 1994 the same company was awarded a similar patent in Europe over soybeans. There is concern that such wide-reaching patents could discourage research by other geneticists into both species and could prevent poor countries from trying to improve these crops and solve local pest problems through genetic engineering.

This problem is not new in science. It has always existed. But it is a bigger problem in genetic engineering than in some other areas of science because research is moving so fast.

Oncomouse

The patent debate did not stop with pieces of DNA. In 1991, the U.S. patent office overruled objections and confirmed its decision to grant a patent on a genetically engineered mouse. Michael Fox of the Humane Society of America called it "an official endorsement that animals...are simple commodities, and are not ours in trust...in a profane world, what else can you expect, where nothing is sacred anymore except human ingenuity." [8]

This mouse carries a death sentence. It is carrying a human gene that makes it prone to cancer. In a short time it will develop the disease and die.

This was no ordinary mouse. Oncomouse, as it is called, carries an implanted human cancer gene in its DNA. This makes it prone to cancer. Cancer researchers can now breed these mice so that each is a walking cancer time bomb. Oncomice are extremely useful, say some scientists. They can be used to test chemicals to see if they might cause cancer in humans. New cancer treatments can also be tested.

Until 1991, scientists had to inject mice with chemicals to give them cancer before they could test their new drugs. This was very artificial. Nobody knew if the tumors were like human tumors. Oncomouse is different because it produces human tumors. But what about Oncomouse? Cancer is a terrible disease, whether you are a human or a mouse.

The U.S. patent office put humans before mice. It ruled that the potential benefit to humans of fighting cancer with the help of oncomouse outweighed the suffering of an animal designed to develop cancer. In early 1993, the European Patent Office agreed. It, too, granted a patent to Harvard University, where Oncomouse was genetically engineered.

Animal rights activists are very unhappy about these decisions. They claim that the Harvard mouse is not as useful as the researchers say. They argue that the animals are so prone to tumors that they are no use in testing chemicals to see if they cause cancer. And they believe that the research that Oncomouse has made possible is not morally desirable.

Should any life be patentable? If geneticists could engineer a laughing mouse, should this be patented like Oncomouse? Where does patenting stop? Doctors have already given new genes to humans. Should these humans be patented, too?

Some people feel very strongly that animals should not be used in scientific experiments. These people are protesting peacefully, but others have vandalized the homes of scientists and even sent them letter bombs.

The Human Genome Project
Oncomouse has raised moral questions about patenting life-forms and about genetically engineering animals so that they develop lethal diseases. The Human Genome

Project, however, has probably caused more controversy among scientists than anyone could have imagined. Again, patent rights have been part of the debate. Some scientists are also unhappy that so much money is being put into one project instead of being more widely spread.

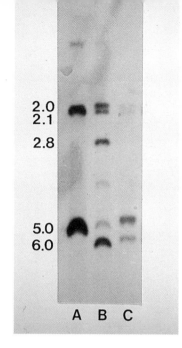

2.0
2.1

2.8

5.0
6.0

A   B   C

Plans for a Human Genome Project were first discussed in the early 1970s. The idea was to map all 100,000 genes on the 46 human chromosomes, collectively known as the human genome. Once they had a map, geneticists believed they would have a much better chance of understanding many of our most common diseases, such as cancer and heart disease, and, hopefully, finding cures for them.

In 1973, when the first human genome meeting was held, only 25 genes had been pinpointed. During the 1980s more and more geneticists across the world agreed to take part in the project. Techniques improved and machines took over a lot of the most laborious work. Progress speeded up. By 1989, 1,656 genes had been mapped. Two years later, the number had jumped by 50 percent—to around 2,500. Hundreds of genes continue to be added each year. The dream of mapping the human genome is fast becoming reality.

One of the most exciting things about the Human Genome Project is that scientists from all over the world are working together toward a common goal. Yet, in 1991, this international cooperation took a big hit. Hope was replaced by suspicion. The National Institutes of Health (NIH) in Bethesda, Maryland, applied for patents on 347 pieces of DNA identified by its researchers. Many researchers on both sides of the Atlantic were horrified.

By the summer of 1992, the NIH had tried to patent some 6,000 pieces of DNA. The British Medical Research Council (MRC) responded by applying for patents on 1,100 fragments.

(Left) Gene by gene, the map of the human genome is being built up. But there is still a long way to go before the picture is complete.

(Below) Some of the equipment used to map the human genome. It is all automated and has dramatically reduced the time it takes to analyze a piece of DNA.

The head of the project, James D. Watson (who had jointly discovered the structure of DNA in the mid 1950s), resigned after many arguments with the NIH.

In September 1992, the U.S. Patent Office rejected the NIH applications on the grounds that the information about the DNA pieces was neither useful nor new. Others agreed that, since no one knows what most of the pieces of DNA do, it would be impossible to patent them because they have no obvious practical use. Peter Goodfellow, Professor of Genetics at Cambridge University in England, explained, "Just having the [fragment] does not tell you anything about the biology. It's just like a land-grab with people saying 'that's mine,' which is silly." [9]

While patents were being considered, geneticists had to keep their discoveries secret. So others wasted time trying to map genes that had already been mapped. Fortunately, in 1994 both sides agreed not to pursue their patent applications. But the Human Genome Project has been damaged by all the bad feeling. The arguments will not prevent all the 100,000 human genes from eventually finding their way onto the map, but no one will know how much sooner the project could have been finished without the patent wars.

The monoclonal antibody

The most important discovery in modern medicine never to be patented was the monoclonal antibody (MAB). In 1975, two Cambridge scientists, Drs. Cesar Milstein and Georges J. F. Koehler, discovered how to make endless amounts of identical antibodies by

A superb view of human chromosomes. The DNA probes, dyed yellow, are used to pick out the genes that the scientists are trying to identify.

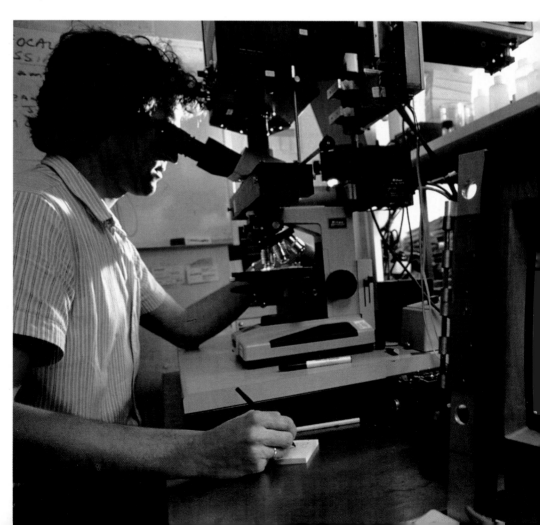

Dr. Cesar Milstein, the scientist who discovered how to clone antibodies. His work has been of immense value to doctors and scientists.

growing a clone of cells from a single cell (hence the name "monoclonal"). Antibodies are molecules that are produced by the body's immune system to fight infection. They home in on proteins called antigens, which act as recognition points on the surface of cells.

Doctors knew that the ability to make large numbers of a single antibody could be very useful in medicine. Because each type of antibody recognizes only a single, specific type of antigen, monoclonal antibodies could be used to identify abnormal proteins in the body, or they could be attached to powerful drugs and used to carry the drugs to diseased cells. Until the Cambridge discovery, there was no way to make monoclonal antibodies in large amounts. Milstein and Koehler changed all that. They fused together cells that made antibodies with cells that live forever. The result was an endless supply of identical monoclonal antibodies.

Milstein and Koehler, along with Niels K. Jerne, were awarded the Nobel Prize for Medicine in 1984, but no one patented their discovery. As a result, British research missed out on a fortune in patent charges. Monoclonal antibodies are now widely used in medicine.

GENETIC PROFILES

Ann and Roger look closely at the pictures that the doctor has put in front of them. Each of the black smudges says something about the genes of Ann and Roger's unborn child. Ann is seventeen weeks pregnant and she is going to have a daughter.

Pregnant women are offered more and more tests to see if their unborn child is growing normally.

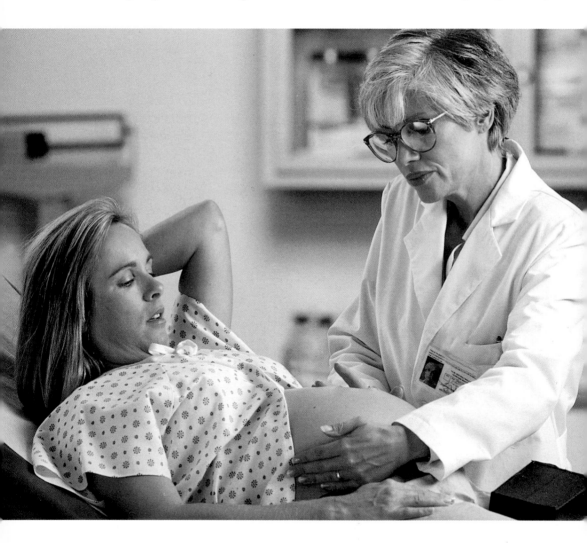

The year is 2010 and, like most parents, Ann and Roger asked for the genetic profile of their daughter. When she was fifteen weeks pregnant, doctors took a blood test from Ann. From her blood they were able to isolate cells from the fetus, which were used to grow more cells in the laboratory. These cells were then tested.

Ann and Roger now have a complete map of their daughter's genes. They can see that she has inherited a tendency toward three diseases: asthma, eczema, and breast cancer. They must make a difficult decision. Do they go on with this pregnancy, or do they abort this fetus and try for a baby who is less likely to get asthma, eczema, or breast cancer?

Roger is familiar with the breathing difficulties caused by asthma, but he takes drugs that control the problem very well. His brother has eczema but, again, drugs keep it under control.

In this ultrasound picture the head of an unborn baby is clearly visible. Close-up pictures of other parts of its body can show whether all its organs have formed correctly.

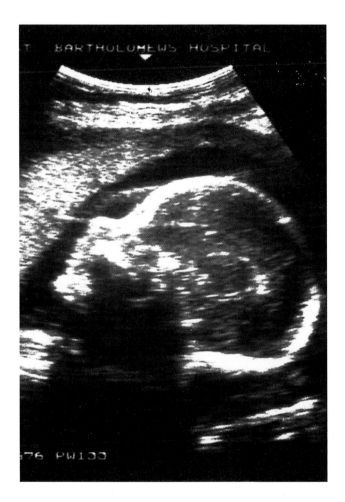

Ann's mother died of breast cancer when she was 42. Her aunt had breast cancer when she was 48, but her treatment seems to have worked. Ann is 35 and knows she is at risk of getting the disease.

Roger and Ann are not worried about having a child who is asthmatic and has some eczema. They have seen that, in their family, these two diseases can be controlled. They feel differently about the risk of breast cancer. Ann saw the effects of breast cancer treatment on her mother and her aunt: it made them both feel very ill. Ann herself must have mammograms once a year. She makes sure she gets plenty of exercise and eats healthily, and she takes hormone tablets every day to help protect her from developing the disease. The tablets sometimes make her feel ill and there is a very small risk that they will eventually damage her liver.

Should Ann and Roger put their daughter through the worry of knowing she could get breast cancer when she is in her early 40s? Like Ann, she will need to take hormone tablets and have mammograms every year.

Ann and Roger's doctor explains the risks and tells them about the research that is going on into breast cancer. Scientists are searching for ways to switch off the gene that makes women prone to the disease. Treatment of breast cancer is also improving. The doctor points out that, if Ann and Roger's daughter does get the disease in her 40s, the year will be 2050. Hopefully, there will be a cure by then.

What should Ann and Roger do? Even if they decide to end this pregnancy there is no guarantee that their next baby would not inherit the same gene. Suppose they find it difficult to have another baby? Ann and Roger think long and hard. In the end they decide to continue the pregnancy and their daughter, Joanna, is born 23 weeks later. She looks fit and healthy. No one can predict her future.

These three youngsters are healthy now, but who knows what is in store for them? In the future, there may be more tests to predict which serious illnesses a child might develop when he or she grows up.

Today's gene tests

Today, parents rarely have to make such difficult decisions. Two out of every hundred children are born with a disease that is caused by a single mutant gene. Yet scientists can only test for some of these diseases.

The most common serious genetic disease is cystic fibrosis. One in twenty people carries the faulty gene. After years of painstaking research, scientists know exactly where the gene is. They have tracked it to chromosome seven.

People with cystic fibrosis make thick mucus in their lungs. This gives them chest infections. Some are also missing important enzymes needed for digestion. Treatment is much better than it used to be, but there is no cure and the disease kills many of its victims.

If a man and woman who both carry the gene for cystic fibrosis have a child, there is a one in four chance that the child will inherit the disease. If the couple know they are both carriers, they can have a prenatal test, as did Ann and Roger, to see if their baby will be affected.

This three-year-old has cystic fibrosis and needs regular physiotherapy to help keep his lungs clear of mucus. A test is now available to find out whether a person carries the disease, and some patients are having gene therapy to try to correct the genetic defect.

However, people rarely know that they are carriers, and many children are born with cystic fibrosis every year. If the parents had known, they might have decided to end the pregnancy.

To test or not?

Some people do not want to know if they have an abnormal gene even when there is a test available. Huntington's chorea is a devastating, incurable mental disease. People gradually become demented, losing control of their mental abilities when they are about 40. Their children have a fifty-fifty chance of inheriting the disease.

There is a test for Huntington's chorea, but many people who are at risk do not want it. Why? If they discover they have the abnormal gene, they must live with the knowledge that they could lose their minds. Nothing can save them. They would prefer not to know.

Alzheimer's disease is a much more common type of mental illness. It usually affects people in their 70s and 80s. Some people who have developed the illness seem to have an abnormal gene. Again, there is no cure, so would people want to be genetically tested for a disease that might affect them years later?

Who should know?

If you could have gene tests for illnesses such as breast cancer, heart disease, and Alzheimer's disease, how would the knowledge that you are likely to develop one of them affect your life? Would you want to know? Who else should have the results of such tests? Your family? Your doctor? Should they be kept officially on computer so anyone could know?

Today, if you want a mortgage or you want some types of insurance, you must answer questions about your health. If you are considered unhealthy—if you have a serious illness such as heart disease, or if you smoke—you may have to pay more. You may even be turned down.

This elderly man is ve[ry] confused and distress[ed.] He has Alzheimer's disease and is losing memory. Eventually h[e] won't even be able to recognize his family. Scientists think they h[ave] found an abnormal ge[ne] that makes some peo[ple] especially prone to Alzheimer's disease.

" "

• • •

A right to privacy?
In its 1993 report, the National Center for Human Genome Research expressed concern about the use of genetic information by insurance companies, especially if the U.S. adopts universal health care coverage: "Our current system erects barriers to health care coverage for people most likely to need it. As information, including genetic information, that predicts individuals' health risks becomes more plentiful, accurate, and inexpensive, those barriers to access will continue to grow, especially for those with the greatest need...Also, the current health care system contains disincentives for people to obtain information about their health risks, including genetic risks...people would be frightened that they would have diminished access to health care coverage." [10]

Imagine what would happen if mortgage and insurance companies had your complete genetic profile. What if a possible employer knew you had genes for heart disease? Would he or she want to take you on? Suppose a university knew you were at risk of developing breast cancer in your early 40s. Would that university want to spend money on training you for several years to become a doctor if you could die only 15 years later?

In some countries, people must have an HIV (human immunodeficiency virus) test before they can get married. This checks whether they have been infected by the HIV virus, which causes AIDS. When we have complete genetic profiles, couples also might want to check each other's genes. Would you want to know if your partner was likely to die young? Would you prefer to look for someone with "healthier" genes?

Would you want information about your health to be stored on a computer so others could check your genes? We need to be sure that there are strict controls on who can see such information.

We are all different. Who is to say which genes are best? Do we want to be able to change our genes or should we be satisfied with the genes with which we are born?

Gene therapy

Four-year-old Amy Harper was one of the first humans to have gene therapy. She was born with a rare immune disorder that kept her body from fighting even the mildest infection. Her white blood cells could not make a vital enzyme.

Gene therapy involves doctors placing a normal, "healthy" gene into cells that have a faulty version of that gene. About one billion of Amy's white cells were removed and the gene for the missing enzyme inserted into the DNA of those cells. The cells were then put back into her body.

Since Amy's treatment in 1991, other children have had gene therapy to correct the same abnormal gene. The children seem to be doing very well, but no one yet knows whether the gene therapy treatment has really been beneficial.

Media Watch

Genetic engineering and the media

Newspaper articles about gene therapy have promised a lot: "The New Attack on Killer Diseases: There's Fresh Hope for Ailments from Cancer to Alzheimer's." [11] Nevertheless, it will be many years before gene therapy becomes routine, and it may yet prove impossible in some conditions. Is it fair to raise people's hopes?

Some newspaper headlines have focused on people's fears: "Geneticists' Latest Discovery: Public Fear of 'Frankenfood'" [12] The ways in which genetic engineering is sometimes presented in the media can make it very difficult for people to decide whether they approve or disapprove.

Another early target for gene therapy was cystic fibrosis. Doctors in several countries, including the United States and Great Britain, developed a way of getting healthy genes into the cells that line the inside of the nose. People with the disease simply sniff the missing genes into their noses. The treatment does not change their own genes, so it has to be repeated every few months.

Many other genetic diseases, including the blood disorder hemophilia

and the muscle-wasting condition Duchenne muscular dystrophy are targets for gene therapy. Some cancers may also respond to this type of treatment.

Getting genes into cells

Viruses have become the unlikely friends of gene therapists. They seem to be the best way to carry normal genes into the cells of people with genetic defects. For thousands of years, viruses have been getting into human cells and causing trouble. Viruses inject their own genes into the human cells, and the viral genes instruct the cells to concentrate all their efforts into making more virus particles. Now the tables are turned, and viruses are helping humans.

First, the viral DNA is carefully treated in the laboratory so that it cannot reproduce itself once it gets into the body. Then, human genes are inserted into the treated viral DNA. This modified viral DNA is put into human cells. It quickly finds its way into the DNA of the cells and the new, healthy gene is soon active. In this way, human cells can be instructed to make a missing protein.

Despite the precautions, scientists are still very nervous about deliberately giving people viruses. In 1993, a U.S. study of gene therapy in cystic fibrosis had to be stopped when a woman given a very large dose of modified virus developed inflammation in her lungs. Scientists had to investigate what had gone wrong.

In Great Britain, scientists using gene therapy to treat cystic fibrosis have avoided viruses. Instead, they have packaged genes into fatty globules. These release the genes into the cells in the nose.

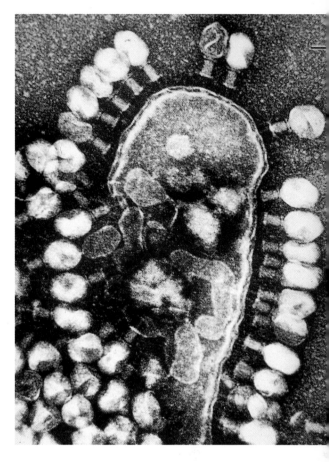

This *E. coli* bacterium is being invaded by viruses. The viruses have symmetrically shaped heads containing their DNA and a single tail that attaches to the wall of the bacterium. The viruses inject their DNA into the bacterium and take it over. (Magnified more than 15,000 times.)

(Left) England's Queen Victoria (seated, center) and family. Some of them, including Victoria, carried the gene for hemophilia and passed on the disease to male children.

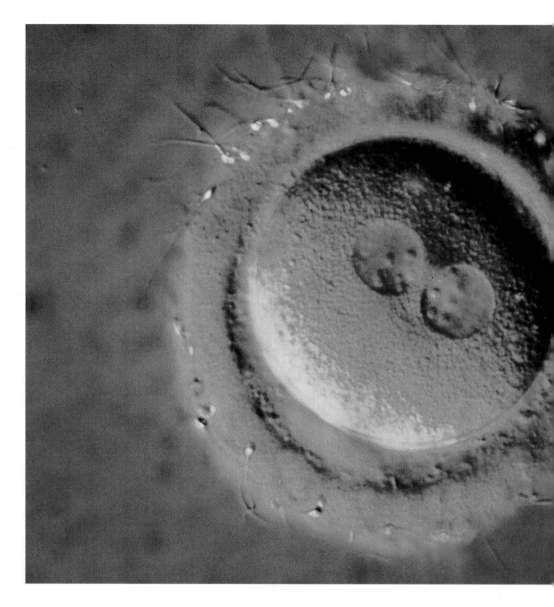

Types of gene therapy

There are two ways to use gene therapy. So far, doctors have been using somatic gene therapy. This means they are changing the genes in ordinary cells, such as those in the lungs or the blood. The person who is treated with somatic gene therapy will, in most cases, still pass on a faulty copy of a gene to his or her children.

Eventually, doctors may want to use germ line therapy. This means changing the genes in human eggs and sperm, and could prevent genetic diseases from being

This human egg has just been fertilized by a male sperm and is starting to divide. Germ line therapy would interfere with the genes in these cells.

passed on by parents to their children. No one knows what long-term effects such changes could have on future generations. Scientists will need to do many more experiments before they try germ line therapy in humans.

Who decides?

Scientists have to get permission to carry out gene therapy in humans. Most leading industrialized countries have special committees, made up of scientists, members of the public, and representatives of religious bodies, to supervise gene therapy procedures. Scientists must tell these committees exactly what they want to do. Only when the committees are satisfied that the experiments are as safe as possible will they give the go-ahead. These committees must also be kept informed of the results of such work and must be told of any problems.

Patients must be asked to take part willingly. Before they agree, the procedure must be explained to them in full so that they understand exactly what is going to happen. They can say no and they can decide to pull out of the experiment at any time.

Children with muscular dystrophy have no mental problems but their muscles are very weak. They need wheelchairs to get around.

NOT ALL IN THE GENES?

When serial killers are sent to prison for life, the judge sometimes refers to them as "wicked" or "evil" in the summing up of the case. What made them so evil? Were they born with genes for wickedness that would inevitably make them murderers ?

Compare such criminals with an international hero or heroine such as Mother Teresa of Calcutta. Was she born with extra genes for "goodness" that led her just as inevitably toward helping the poor and disadvantaged?

When gene therapy becomes a routine part of medical care, will doctors be able to turn us into nicer, kinder people as well as healthier ones? If it should prove possible, should we expect scientists to cure people of antisocial behavior in the same way as they correct faulty genes that cause physical diseases?

Jeffrey L. Dahmer at his first court appearance in 1991. He was later convicted of killing fifteen young men. Did he choose to commit evil acts? Had he developed psychological problems? Or was he was "born evil?"

For decades, geneticists have found it impossible to agree on how important our genes are in deciding whether we grow up good or bad, happy or sad, gentle or aggressive, creative or logical, and how important other factors are, such as the environment in which we grow up. They call it the "nature versus nurture" controversy.

Even the finest musicians need help and encouragement to make the most of their talents.

A boy may be born with great musical talent, but no one will ever know this if he never listens to music or goes near a musical instrument. A girl may be born with a gift for mathematics, but she is unlikely to use that skill if she does not go to school.

Even if gene differences that give us particular talents were found, they would not be enough on their own to make us take advantage of those talents. We need to learn how to use them. Tennis stars Steffi Graf and Pete Sampras may have been born with particular physical strengths and with a natural ability for eye-hand coordination. Nevertheless, they became champions only through thousands of hours of hard practice over many years. If they do not play for a few months, they lose the extra skill that makes them winners, and they have to practice more to reach the top again.

From a very early age we are influenced by what we see around us. A child who grows up in war-torn Bosnia is surrounded by people with guns. So, at age seven or eight, this child may also carry a gun. This does not mean the child was born with genes that have created a killer. He or she uses a gun because it appears to be normal behavior.

Sadly, parents who physically abuse their children are often found to have been abused themselves when they were children. Have they inherited abuse genes from their parents or are they simply copying what they thought was normal when they were children?

During the 1930s and 1940s, Nazi leaders in Germany had a very simplistic view of genetics. They believed

This Nazi propaganda poster from the 1930s shows a girl of the fair-skinned or "Aryan" appearance the Nazis favored. The Nazis took their belief in racial purity to the extreme, and they killed those who were not "Aryans" or who disagreed with their views.

that if they "purified" the German population by breeding only among those with the fair-skinned appearance of northern Europeans, they would become a "super race" with all the physical and mental characteristics that they admired. They were sure that genes controlled behavior.

Good health is only partly inherited. If parents encourage their children to exercise, then they are more likely to grow up fit and healthy.

After World War II, the "nurture" view grew in popularity in the West. Upbringing was felt to be more important than genes. Children who were brought up in happy, loving families were expected to grow into good, law-abiding citizens. An unhappy home life or divorced parents were generally blamed when children dropped out of school or got into trouble with the police. Yet some children who were brought up in happy homes still became criminals, and most of those who lived in bad conditions never broke the law.

Human beings inherit all manner of factors that affect how they develop both physically and mentally. We are influenced by such things as the availability, or lack, of money; a good or bad diet; parents who smoke when their children are around; and the beliefs and attitudes of our parents. It is hard to see how these things can be separated. Over the last two decades opinion has continued to swing back and forth between the nature and nurture theories.

A gene for aggression?

No one has found genes for goodness or evil but, in 1993, Dutch scientists wrote about an aggressive family, some members of which seemed to have a defective gene on their X chromosome. Many male members of the family over several generations were found to have a history of violent behavior, and some had mild learning disabilities.

Genetic tests showed that these men had an abnormal gene on their X chromosome. The X chromosome is one of the chromosomes that determines the sex of a person. Women have two X chromosomes (XX) and men have an X chromosome and a Y chromosome (XY). Men always inherit their single X chromosome from their mothers.

The gene that is at fault in the aggressive men normally encodes for an enzyme that breaks down chemicals that carry messages between nerves in the brain. Without the enzyme, large quantities of these chemicals build up and cannot be removed. High levels of these chemicals have previously been found in aggressive animals.

Chromosomes from a man's cells. They are the same as a woman's cells except for the X and Y chromosomes (bottom right). A woman has two identical X chromosomes; a man has one X and one Y. (Magnified over 1,000 times.)

Some newspapers announced that scientists had discovered the "aggression" gene, but there were also voices of caution: "The notion that an 'aggressive' gene has been found is as yet premature. It may be that [a change in] this gene is responsible for one in a million cases of aggression in the general population." [13] So far, the indication that there might be a connection between aggression and a gene has been found in only the one Dutch family.

Is a predisposition toward violence a result of genetics or environment? Partly because of the belief it may be caused by environment, video stores are not allowed to rent R- or X-rated videos to people under 18. But some children still manage to see violent films that many adults would not want them to watch.

At around the same time, a series of murders in England was blamed on the influence of horror movies on videotape. The murderers were known to have watched some very violent movies before killing people. There is no evidence that they came from violent families.

Contrast this with the case of the five-year-old Indian boy who beat three other children to death in 1993 for no apparent reason. He had never seen a television, let alone a horror movie. Again, there was no history of violence in his family.

Is it possible to blame all violence or wickedness on our genes or on our environment? Surely we must take some responsibility for our own actions. How can we tell what makes people commit terrible crimes?

Sexual orientation

For many years, scientists have been trying to understand why some people are heterosexual and others are homosexual. Do our sexual preferences depend on our genes or on the way we grow up?

These gay men are open about their sexuality, but gays and lesbians still face discrimination.

In 1991, scientists in California found that a tiny part of the brain, which they believe is responsible for sexual behavior, is smaller in women and in homosexual men than in heterosexual men. This was the first time that a genuine physical difference between homosexuals and heterosexuals had been found. In July 1993, another group of U.S. scientists announced that they had discovered a gene on the X chromosome that was more common in families where several members were homosexual, particularly on the mother's side of the family. However, the study that led to the discovery was thrown into question. People had jumped upon the idea that inheriting this particular piece of DNA on the X chromosome was the main cause of homosexuality. Yet it may be that a mother's pattern of behavior, determined by that gene, affects the development of the sexual orientation of her children.

Finding a gene for homosexuality might be thought helpful to those homosexuals who feel guilty for religious or other reasons about their sexual orientation. It would mean they need not blame themselves for being gay. However, it is worrying for those who believe it could lead to prenatal gene tests for homosexuality. Even if the genetic link is proven, would it be right for couples to be offered abortion of a fetus with the gene, as they would be for a fetus with the cystic fibrosis or muscular dystrophy gene?

66   99

• • •

Genes and sexuality
Even when a gene is identified—such as the one that appeared to be linked to homosexuality—geneticists must then find out how it works: "Sexual orientation is too complex to be determined by a single gene, [but] the main value of this work is that it opens a window into understanding how genes, the brain, and the environment interact to mold human behavior." [14]

Who is to judge which versions of genes are socially acceptable and which are not? If we aim to reduce the number of children born with physical or mental disabilities, who is to decide where the line should be drawn? From reducing the number of disabled people in society, might we move toward reducing the number of people who simply do not conform to our ideas of normal behavior? This could just as well include the highly gifted, eccentric recluse as the disadvantaged petty criminal.

" "

• • •

Genetics and society
The possibility that homosexuality may be genetic raises questions about how society should respond to such a discovery: "The political implications of this could be very negative. It emphasizes the need for ethical controls, otherwise this could be seriously abused. It would be a very retrograde step if people terminated pregnancies—what we need is change in attitudes to gay people, not ways of eliminating them." [15]

Some of the most severely disabled people in our community also have some of the most remarkable gifts. The British physicist Stephen Hawking can neither speak nor move unaided because of a serious neurological condition.

You can't tell a genius from a petty criminal by looking at them. Who knows what these people will do when they grow up?

A painting illustrating autism. Autistic children cannot communicate by speech, and they become isolated. Autism is very rare, affecting two to four children out of every 10,000.

Yet his theories about the shaping of the universe have had an important effect on scientific thinking.

Some children with autism—a condition that imprisons people in their own inner world, unable to communicate with others—have remarkable artistic or mathematical abilities or other talents.

By trying to design perfect humans, we could be in danger of losing these and other great talents that enrich our society. The very diversity of the human species could be one reason it has been successful.

Some scientists are promising us "designer" children—but do we want them? Do we want genetic engineering to turn us into a society that finds anyone with unusual physical or mental characteristics unacceptable? Does genetic engineering really have this potential? If environment is as important as our genes in deciding how we turn out, the search for a "best set of genes" may well be pointless anyway—the effects of these genes on each individual would be affected by different environmental factors, not just in childhood but throughout life.

RELIVING THE PAST

When the man-eating raptors got loose in *Jurassic Park,* no one was safe.

If the record-breaking film *Jurassic Park* had been released ten years ago, we would all have known it was just a great science fiction story with dazzling effects. Today, however, we have much greater expectations and people find themselves asking, "Could we really bring dinosaurs back from extinction?"

In the film, scientists cloned tyrannosaurs, stegosaurs, raptors, and other dinosaurs from preserved DNA samples and put them in a theme park. Some of the most dangerous species escaped and caused havoc before they were eventually killed.

In reality, no one has yet cloned an extinct species, but scientists have managed to extract fragments of DNA from them. In February 1992, there was a report that blood from a 100,000-year-old Neanderthal human had been found on a primitive tool in Iraq. This was an important discovery: it gave scientists the chance to look at prehistoric DNA and search for similarities to DNA from modern humans.

> " "
> • • •
>
> **Learning from the past**
> The finding of a blood sample from a Neanderthal man raised high hopes: "The only way we are going to discover the truth about recent evolutionary past is by studying ancient blood samples like this one. It is not just an academic exercise. Our evolution has been heavily influenced by our ability to survive diseases such as malaria. Our future may depend on us surviving other, even deadlier epidemics. We have a lot to learn about ourselves. Our past is a very important window on our future." [16]

A month later, in March 1992, news came that scientists had isolated DNA from a bee embedded in amber for 25 million years. It was the oldest DNA ever found. This made scientists very excited. They had been finding it impossible to extract DNA from bones more than 50,000 years old because of the decay caused by lying in the ground for so long. Now, they had found a material—amber—that appeared to preserve DNA much better.

This midge, an ancestor of today's mosquitoes, has been embedded in amber for about 40 million years. Amber is a sticky resin that oozes from dead trees and hardens into a fossil. An insect can be preserved for millions of years if it is trapped in amber. (Magnified over 10 times.)

Scientists don't expect to find dinosaur bones preserved in amber—they would be too big. Just as happened in *Jurassic Park*, however, they might find the body of an insect that had bitten a dinosaur or other extinct animal. They would be unlikely to get a complete piece of dinosaur DNA. Nevertheless, they could extend some sections by making copies in the laboratory, and they could fill in some missing pieces with DNA from a modern species with similar-looking DNA.

Dinosaurs became extinct about 65 million years ago, so scientists will have to find amber samples much older than those they have discovered so far. Even so, they may still find there is too much DNA missing for them to attempt a serious recreation of a dinosaur.

Condors are on the verge of extinction.

Genetic archaeologists are not only targeting dinosaurs. They are looking at DNA from species that died out much more recently—animals such as the woolly mammoth, which became extinct only about 10,000 years ago. With these animals, they can expect to find samples of DNA with fewer pieces missing.

Animals that are currently on the verge of extinction may offer the most exciting genetic possibilities. Zoologists have complete samples of DNA from species such as the rhinoceros, tiger, and condor, and they are able to preserve the DNA until they have the technology to produce clones.

Of course, if we want these animals to live and breed again in their old hunting grounds of Africa, Southeast Asia, and South America, we will need to preserve their habitats, too. The disappearance of the rain forests and savannas would be just as catastrophic to any future generations of cloned tigers, elephants, lions, and rhinos as it is to today's natural inhabitants.

We would need to ask ourselves what effect the reintroduction of extinct species would have on our environment. Some species simply may not be able to survive in today's world, and are we certain we could live easily alongside animals from the past?

"The Four-Sided Triangle" by William F. Temple was a story published in 1939. In it, a woman was cloned so that the two men who loved her could each have a copy.

Cloning humans

In 1978, a book was published called *In His Image: The Cloning of a Man* by David M. Rorvik. It claimed to be the true account of the cloning of a man. In fact, it wasn't true—the story was made up. Scientists concluded that such a thing was impossible.

In October 1993, however, U.S. scientists announced that they had cloned human embryos. They took 17 abnormal eggs, with three sets of chromosomes instead of the usual two, and split them. They coated each with a protective membrane similar to that which is normally found around an embryo and watched them grow. Several did, though none was put into a woman's womb. In the end, they all died.

This cloning experiment was different from that described in the Rorvik book, which used a single, ordinary cell from a man to create a child. In the recent experiment, an egg fertilized by a sperm was split to form a copy. This is similar to what happens naturally when identical twins are formed.

Even so, some scientists were horrified by the cloning experiment. They argued that cloning had no advantage over current techniques used for test-tube babies to help infertile couples have children. It could, however, lead to scientists trying to clone humans from single cells taken from the skin or some other tissue. It could mean that clones could be stored as potential organ donors. Yet most people believe that cloning humans would be undesirable.

Many identical twins have to struggle all their lives to develop identities of their own.

Many people might support the cloning of animals on the verge of extinction. Cloning can produce large numbers of genetically identical offspring relatively quickly. But who would agree to the cloning of humans?

As with all of the exciting advances in genetic engineering discussed in this book, it is up to us to make clear what our ethics will allow, rather than just accepting what is scientifically possible. All too often in the past, public debate has followed, not preceded, a major medical or scientific advance. Once something has been done it is very hard to undo it.

Most leading scientists involved in genetic engineering want people to understand what is happening in their laboratories and how their work could affect our lives. For example, the U.S. Human Genome Project has been spending $5 million a year since 1990 to encourage public discussion and to support research to anticipate the social impact of the science it sponsors. When scientists open their doors we must help to decide what should go on inside.

This researcher is taking samples of cells from a gene bank. Each tube contains about one million cells. Scientists will study them to find the genes that cause inherited diseases.

MILESTONES TO GENETIC ENGINEERING

1859	Charles Darwin published his revolutionary theories about evolution in *On the Origin of Species by Means of Natural Selection.*
1866	Gregor Johann Mendel published his theories of genetic inheritance.
1902	Walter Sutton linked chromosomes with Mendel's theories of genetics.
1909	Wilhelm Johannsen introduced the term *gene.*
Early 1940s	Accumulated evidence showed that DNA must be the carrier of genetic information.
1953	James Watson and Francis Crick discovered the structure of DNA.
1960	Arthur Kornberg reported he had made DNA in the laboratory.
1961	François Jacob and Jacques Monod proposed the means by which genes regulate each other through particular "regulator" genes.
1973	Stanley Cohen and Herbert Boyer reported the first successful genetic engineering experiments.
1974	Geneticists called for a temporary ban on genetic engineering experiments until safety had been considered.
1977	The first human hormone was made in a bacterial cell.
1980	U.S. scientist David Botstein made a rough genome map.
1990	First human gene therapy trial initiated by Dr. W. French Anderson at the National Institutes of Health, Bethesda, Maryland. Human Genome Project officially began.
1993	Genetic mutation for Huntington's chorea identified.
1994	Dr. Mark H. Skolnick's team at the University of Utah Medical Center found a gene they believe causes breast cancer.

GLOSSARY

AIDS (Acquired Immune Deficiency Syndrome) A disease believed to be caused by the human immunodeficiency virus (HIV). Sufferers lose the ability to fight infection; eventually, this leads to death.

Alzheimer's disease A disease causing slow loss of memory and the ability to think.

amber A hard, clear, yellowish substance formed from trees that have been dead for millions of years.

amino acids Simple organic units in living things. They link together to make proteins.

antibody A molecule produced by the body to fight infection.

asthma A disease that causes narrowing of the airways in the lungs, making it hard to breathe.

autism A mental condition. Sufferers withdraw into themselves and are unable to communicate with others.

bacterium (plural bacteria) A type of single-celled microorganism that can live in animals or plants or on its own. Some bacteria cause disease.

cell The smallest living part of any living thing. Animals have millions of cells that do many different jobs. Cells can be grown and kept alive in the laboratory for long periods.

chromosome A threadlike structure found in the nucleus of animal and plant cells. It is made up of DNA (which carries the genes) and protein. Humans have 23 pairs of chromosomes, including a pair of sex chromosomes.

clone To make identical copies without sexual reproduction. In genetic engineering, it is common to clone a gene, an antibody or a cell.

cystic fibrosis The most common serious genetic disease; it affects the lungs and intestines.

DNA (deoxyribonucleic acid) A substance in nearly all living things that forms the structure of genes. In animals and plants, the DNA is found in the chromosomes.

domesticated Tamed or brought under control to live and work with humans.

Duchenne muscular dystrophy A genetic disorder that causes muscles to waste away in boys and is usually fatal in adolescence.

eczema A condition that makes the skin dry, itchy, red, and sore.

embryo A developing organism; in humans it describes the unborn child between two and eight weeks after the egg is fertilized by a sperm.

enzyme A protein that speeds up chemical reactions in the body.

ethical Concerned with the rights and wrongs of human behavior.

factor VIII A substance that makes the blood clot; people who do not have factor VIII in their blood (hemophiliacs) can bleed to death unless they get medical treatment.

gene A section of DNA that carries the instructions for making an enzyme or other protein.

gene therapy Attempting to cure genetic diseases by placing a normal gene into cells that have a faulty version of that gene.

genetic code The way in which messages for protein are "written" in DNA.

genetic engineering The deliberate alteration of a living thing by modifying its DNA and changing its genetic makeup.

genetic fingerprinting A method of identifying an individual by looking at the unique patterns in his or her DNA.

geneticist An expert who studies genes and heredity.

genome All the genes of an organism.

hemophilia A genetic disease that causes severe bleeding from even a small injury because the blood cannot clot normally.

heterosexual A person who is sexually attracted to people of the opposite sex.

homosexual A person who is sexually attracted to people of the same sex.

hormones Substances in plants and animals that help cells function properly.

FURTHER READING

Huntington's chorea A genetic disease that usually starts in one's 40s and leads to the loss of mental abilities.

microbe Any type of microorganism, including bacteria and viruses.

monoclonal antibody A single-celled antibody that can be made in large amounts in a laboratory by cloning.

naturalist An expert who studies animal and plant life.

Neanderthal man An early type of human living in Europe from about 125,000 B.C.

nucleus (plural nuclei) The central part of a cell; it controls the cell's functions and contains the chromosomes.

Oncomouse A type of mouse genetically engineered to be prone to cancer.

patent The right to make, use, or sell an invention or discovery. A patent is given by a government and means that anyone wanting to make use of the invention or discovery must pay the owner of the patent a fee.

peptide Two or more amino acids linked together.

plasmid A piece of DNA found outside the nucleus of a cell. Also used in genetic engineering to transfer genes into foreign cells.

predisposition a particular inclination of mind or character.

primate An animal belonging to the group of most complex mammals, called the Primates. The group includes monkeys and humans.

protein A large molecule made of hundreds or thousands of amino acids. Proteins are essential to all living things.

savanna A grassy plain with few or no trees.

serial killer Someone who murders repeatedly.

virus A microorganism, much smaller than a bacterium. It reproduces itself inside the cells of the organism it invades and often causes disease.

Crick, Francis. *What Mad Pursuit: A Personal View of Scientific Discovery.* New York: Basic Books, 1990.

Davis, Bernard. *The Genetic Revolution: Scientific Prospects and Public Perceptions.* Baltimore: Johns Hopkins University Press, 1991.

Dudley, William, ed. *Genetic Engineering: Opposing Viewpoints.* San Diego: Greenhaven, 1990.

Edelson, Edward. *Genetics and Heredity.* The Encyclopedia of Health. New York: Chelsea House, 1991.

Huxley, Aldous. *Brave New World.* New York: HarperPerennials, 1932.

Lampton, Christopher. *DNA Fingerprinting.* Impact Books. New York: Franklin Watts, 1991.

Miller, Jonathan and Van Loon, Borin. *Darwin for Beginners.* New York: Pantheon, 1982.

Tudge, Colin. *The Engineer in the Garden: Genes and Genetics.* New York: Hill & Wang, 1994.

Watson, James. *The Double Helix.* New York: Dutton/Signet, 1969.

Notes on sources

1 Paul Berg et al, *Science*, vol.185, p.303, 1974.
2 Dick Russell, *The Amicus Journal*, Spring 1993, vol. 15, no. 1, p. 23.
3 Bernard E. Rollin, director of bioethical planning, Colorado State University, *USA Today* magazine, November 1990.
4 Jeremy Rifkin, The Pure Food Campaign, "Frankenstein's Tomatoes," *Daily Telegraph*, November 7, 1992.
5 Bill Hiatt, Calgene, "Frankenstein's Tomatoes," *Daily Telegraph*, November 7, 1992.
6 Professor Alec Jeffreys, *The Independent on Sunday*, July, 22,1990.
7 Report by the National Academy of Sciences' Committee on DNA Technology in Forensic Science, as quoted by *The New York Times*, April 14, 1992.
8 Michael Fox, Humane Society of America, *The Independent*, November 17, 1988.
9 Peter Goodfellow, Cambridge University, *New Scientist*, November 6, 1993.
10 "Genetic Information and Health Insurance: Report of the Task Force on Genetic Information and Insurance," The National Institutes of Health, National Center for Human Genome Research, May 10, 1993, p. 9.
11 *Fortune*, April 22, 1991, p. 181.
12 *New York Times*, June 28, 1992.
13 Gregory Carey, University of Colorado, *New Scientist*, October 30, 1993.
14 Dr. Dean Hamer of the National Cancer Institute, quoted in the July 16th, 1993 *New York Times*.
15 Dr. John Bancroft, Medical Research Council Reproductive Biology Unit, Edinburgh, *Daily Telegraph*, July 16, 1993.
16 Dr. Thomas Loy, Australian National University, *The Observer*, February 9, 1992.

INDEX